Those Innocent Years

Those Innocent Years

1898-1914

Images of the Jersey Shore from The Pach Photographic Collection

George H. Moss Jr.

Karen L. Schnitzspahn

Ploughshare Press

Sea Bright, New Jersey

GEORGE JAY MORRIS
1901-1970

a photographer
a fisherman
a friend

George – we finally did it.

FIRST EDITION
Copyright © 1993 by George H. Moss Jr.
Library of Congress Catalogue Card Number: 93-84407
ISBN: 0-912396-06-7
Printed in the United States of America

LIMITED SOFT COVER EDITION
Copyright © 1997 by George H. Moss Jr.
ISBN: 0-912396-08-3
Printed in the United States of America

Table of Contents

Foreword VI

Preface VIII

The Pach Photographers XII

CHAPTER ONE
Portraits – formal and informal 1

CHAPTER TWO
The Changing Scene 29

CHAPTER THREE
Leisure Time Activities 57

CHAPTER FOUR
The Business Community 87

CHAPTER FIVE
The Automobile Comes of Age 115

Foreword

It has often been said that a picture is worth more than a thousand words and the camera in its exactness brings back memories of a time long past. The proud accomplishments of Americans and their social life has been brought into sharp focus by George H. Moss Jr. and Karen L. Schnitzspahn. Through their research this book will now preserve an unforgettable group of images for future generations.

When the new art of photography reached America in the fall of 1839, the Frenchman Daguerre's invention was quickly improved by American entrepreneurs so that portraits from life could be taken and the spirit of an age be recorded for posterity.

After the Civil War, many photographers roamed about country and seaside in the summertime. By following the crowds to resorts, they often combined business with pleasure and captured memorable scenes of America at play.

It was during this period that the young Pach Brothers opened a photography studio at Long Branch, New Jersey. "The Branch" was an excellent summer resort for a photographer to record all of the exciting doings of both the prominent people and the average American enjoying a holiday. The money moguls came, and political bigwigs, artists and actors were likewise drawn to this great resort. President Grant at his seaside cottage was a big attraction as was the popular actress Maggie Mitchell, a longtime resident of Long Branch.

By the turn of the century, the New Jersey Coast had become a favorite vacation spot for the elite. Every major metropolitan newspaper's society column had references to Rumson, Sea Bright, Monmouth Beach, Long Branch, Elberon, Asbury Park, Spring Lake and Lakewood where the social leaders held their gatherings. Sea Bright and Long Branch, with their large ornate hotels enjoyed an international reputation for food and service to entice the wealthy vacationer. Asbury Park, with its many hotels and a variety of attractions was often host to thousands of daily summer visitors.

This was an exciting age of change even though it was an age of innocence. Emerging from the Victorian years and moving into the early twentieth century, people enjoyed newfound leisure time. The automobile was a challenging innovation that soon became part of the American tradition. It was an era of new horizons and that change can be found in the revealing pages of this new book.

We were more than pleased when asked to write the Foreword for *Those Innocent Years*. Both of us grew up along the Jersey Coast and are natives of New Jersey. We remember stories told by our parents and grandparents about the era that the Pach photographs illustrate in this book. World War I would bring that period to and end. It would be followed by the flapper age of the Roaring Twenties – but that would be another story.

Having written more than a dozen books and articles on nineteenth century photography and social history that were illustrated by photographs from the daguerreotype era onward, we feel a close affinity to the portraits and scenes illustrated in *Those Innocent Years*. We also recognize the time, dedication and decisions needed to produce a pictorial history such as this.

George H. Moss Jr. and Karen L. Schnitzspahn are to be commended for their selection of photographs and their research, editing and attention to detail which has resulted in this delightful book. In *Those Innocent Years*, they have successfully documented a period of life at the Jersey Shore that may have otherwise been lost to future generations.

Floyd and Marion Rinhart
Ft. Pierce, Florida

Floyd and Marion Rinhart are noted collectors and authorities of early photographic techniques and have authored a variety of books on both early photography and 19th century social history. As lecturing professors, they have conducted seminars on both subjects at The Ohio State University, the University of Georgia and the National Society for Photographic Education. Their collections of early photographic images, now housed at Ohio State, are nationally recognized.

Preface

A photograph is a mirror of a moment. It is also considered to be among the most valuable of all the documents of history.

As a picture historian and a fourth generation resident of the Jersey Shore, I have sought to preserve this area's pictorial history for over fifty years. My interest in the photographic documentation of the Jersey Shore resulted, three decades ago, in a fortunate discovery and major acquisition of thousands of original glass plate negatives made between 1898 and 1914.

These fragile negatives vary from 5x7 inches to 20x24 inches in size. They are superb examples of the work of two exceptional and highly respected photographers – G.W. Pach (who started business in Long Branch in the 1860's) and his co-worker and eventual successor in New Jersey, George A. M. Morris.

The significance of this collection lies in the preservation, on film, of many outdoor recreational and summertime activities found at the Jersey Shore just a few generations ago. Of equal importance is the preservation of the images of men, women and children as they enjoyed the lifestyle of that bygone era.

The photographs reproduced from Morris and Pach's negatives reflect the exceptional quality of their work. Each carefully selected photograph represents a mere heartbeat, a fleeting moment in time, yet captures the essence of those halcyon moments between the end of one war and the beginning of another – *Those Innocent Years*.

In 1971, I wrote *Double Exposure – Early Stereographic Views of Historic Monmouth County, New Jersey and Their Relationship to Pioneer Photography*. That book, with an introduction by Carlin Gasteyer of the Museum of the City of New York, documented three-dimensional photographs of the Jersey Shore made between 1859 and 1889. *Those Innocent Years* preserves, photographically, yet another portion of Monmouth County's history.

Those Innocent Years is the result of a chance meeting in the summer of 1963, at a local marina, with George Jay Morris. A successful industrial photographer for over thirty years, he was the son of the late George A. M. Morris, also a superb photographer. "Young George" received national acclaim in 1942 for his work on a series of patriotic photographic portraits for Liggett and Myers Tobacco Company's Chesterfield advertisements.

My father was an acquaintance of George A. M. Morris in Long Branch in 1908. Many times I heard him praise Morris for his skill as a photographer. I often wondered what happened to all the negatives the elder Morris made through the years. "Young George" told me those that had survived two fires many years earlier were stored in his mother's garage in Long Branch.

With much anticipation I accepted George's invitation to meet at that garage on the following weekend. There, he showed me a collection of nearly fifteen thousand glass plate negatives. Made by his father, George A. M. Morris, and G. W. Pach, each negative was stored vertically on shelves in its original paper sleeve. All were appropriately identified and filed numerically.

I was astonished by the quality of the work. The beautifully exposed negatives and the pristine sharpness of the images were an exciting revelation.

The variety of subjects was an unexpected surprise: exterior and interior views of sumptuous thirty-room "cottages," boardwalk and beach scenes, hotels and business establishments, baseball, boating, bowling, golf, tennis, polo, horse shows, air shows, automobiles and people. People – thousands of formal and informal portraits of individuals, families, groups and organizations. Often recognizable faces from the past including Mark Twain, Sir Thomas Lipton, politicians, generals, summer visitors and earlier generations of many families who still live at the Jersey Shore. Two earlier generations of my own family were represented in photographs I had never seen.

All around me was an unprecedented pictorial record of almost sixteen summers at the Jersey Shore. Captured by the camera's eye and preserved for all time were previous generations in the midst of lighthearted outdoor summer activities in the Highlands, Sea Bright, Rumson, Monmouth Beach, Long Branch, Elberon, Deal, Allenhurst, Asbury Park, Avon, Belmar, Spring Lake and Lakewood.

Spanning a dozen years, five hundred negatives of financier George Jay Gould and his family at their Lakewood, New Jersey, home were a treasure trove unto themselves.

My deep personal interest in all the negatives was obvious and George Jay Morris understood. Two institutions, a commercial archive and a city library, had previously looked at this collection. George indicated to me he really preferred the collection remain in the area. A few weeks later we reached an agreement and I acquired the thousands of negatives plus the studio registers, photographic lenses, some camera and darkroom equipment, hundreds of magnificent original photographic prints and all the surviving corporate business records of George A. M. Morris.

After a careful inspection, "Young George" and I agreed with the determination noted by the interested institutions: preservation, storage and cataloging were major considerations in acquiring the collection. I finally selected only five thousand significant negatives – mostly outdoor views and certain exceptional portraits.

Using the studio registers as guides, it took over three weeks to sort through the entire collection. With help from my friend, William Alter, we removed the five thousand negatives of my choice. THAT, I might add, was like transporting the world's largest greenhouse, glass pane by glass pane!

I have named this acquisition the "Pach Collection" simply because many of the negatives had their beginning at G. W. Pach's Lakewood studio in 1898.

As an experienced amateur photographer I was delighted with George's later visits to my darkroom. He shared with me his knowledge and technique of fine photographic print making from those fragile negatives. George, a splendid surf fisherman of the old school, also took the time to show my young son George the art of custom-making his own saltwater fishing rods. Today, he carries on that Morris tradition.

I am grateful to Oscar White, president of Pach Brothers, New York, for his friendship. More than twenty-five years ago he graciously printed a number of photographs from my Pach Collection of New Jersey negatives. The prints were an inspiration and have remained an unequaled standard of excellence.

Most importantly, I wish to thank Karen L. Schnitzspahn for joining me as co-author in this latest work to preserve the pictorial history of the Jersey Shore. Our common interest in both early photographic images and the Victorian Era, coupled with her talent for writing and research and her discerning eye for detail, has made this a pleasant task.

George H. Moss Jr.

ABOUT THE PHOTOGRAPHS

They are unretouched contact prints made from glass plate negatives taken between 1898 and 1914. Either 5x7, 8x10 or 11x14 inches in size, they were printed on Eastman Kodak Polycontrast III RC paper between 1990 and 1992.

Each photograph, carefully chosen for both interest and importance, is identified by the original number and name found in the studio registers. Sufficient negatives were dated allowing a majority of photographs to be placed in a reasonable proper time frame. In most instances it was even possible to identify the location of outdoor subjects.

With certain exceptions, the photographs have not been seen since they were first taken more than eighty years ago. Some of the general views of the area, historically significant today, were commercial photographs originally made for Central Railroad of New Jersey promotional brochures and booklets. A number of Pach/Morris photographs were also taken expressly for early publishers of shore area souvenir booklets, while others were produced for use by major postcard companies.

The majority of photographs in the Pach Collection, however, were commissioned by individuals or families. These are the pictures of treasured moments – of special events – that touched the lives of this particular generation. A wedding, a new car, a child with a toy, a family portrait – those all important memories have survived on film for yet another generation.

The five chapters of *Those Innocent Years* i.e. Portraits – formal and informal, The Changing Scene, Leisure Time Activities, The Business Community and The Automobile Comes of Age, were a logical and natural style of presentation. Selected from hundreds of other significant prints, the specific choice of only a few illustrations for those individual chapters, nevertheless, was quite difficult. Because of their subject matter, many photographs fell into more than one category thus creating even more difficult decisions. Altogether, the photographs in this book represent but a sample of what the Pach Collection is all about.

ACKNOWLEDGEMENTS

Acknowledgements and thanks are due Oscar White, Rose Pach, Alfred Pach III, J. Dallas Badrow, Herbert A. Wisbey, Jr., Randall Gabrielan and Muriel Scoles. In their own way, they have each contributed to this book through valuable insight and information.

Also, sincere appreciation to Floyd and Marion Rinhart, for generously consenting to write the foreword to *Those Innocent Years*.

Our very special thanks go to Mary Alice Moss and Leon Schnitzspahn for their patience and understanding.

March, 1993

George H. Moss Jr
Karen L. Schnitzspahn

The Pach Photographers

The scope of the Pach photographers' work is astounding. They photographed everything from formal portraits of celebrities to informal shots of everyday people, from scenes of luxurious estates to views of modest homes and shops. The Pach studios of the late nineteenth and early twentieth century were thriving commercial enterprises operating not only at several Jersey Shore resorts and New York City, but also at strategic locations including college towns in New York, New Jersey, Pennsylvania and New England.

The firm of Pach Brothers, known as "Photographers to the Presidents" – having photographed every chief executive from Ulysses S. Grant to Richard M. Nixon – could also be called "Photographers to the Jersey Shore." Pach cameramen documented life in Monmouth and Ocean Counties for almost fifty years.

Gustavus W. Pach and his brother, Gotthelf, opened their first photo studio at the seashore resort of Long Branch, New Jersey, in 1867. Their success soon prompted them to expand to New York City and other locations. In 1903, G. W. Pach retired from the New York studio and bought out the New Jersey operations at Long Branch and Lakewood. Although the Jersey Shore firm ceased to exist by the start of the First World War, Pach Brothers of New York is still in business today.

Born in Berlin in 1845, Gustavus W. Pach emigrated to America with his family at an early age. He was an apprentice with D. Appleton Co., a notable New York City photographic firm of the

Gustavus W. Pach.

Gotthelf Pach.

time. When he was fifteen years old, Gustavus developed respiratory problems and doctors gave him only a year to live. He was sent to Toms River, New Jersey, to benefit from the country air in the then-rustic Ocean County area known for its healthy environment. He recuperated and continued to pursue a career in photography.

During the summer of 1866, G.W. Pach, in his early twenties, and his younger brother, Gotthelf, were taking orders for photographs out of a cigar store at Long Branch and using a wagon as a mobile studio. Set upon a picturesque bluff overlooking the Atlantic Ocean, Long Branch was one of the nation's most popular watering places and attracted many wealthy vacationers from New York and Philadelphia.

The following summer, the Pach brothers had an opportunity to use their photographic talents at the lavish summer "cottage" of Philadelphia publisher George W. Childs. The details of exactly what happened that day are uncertain. Apparently, Gustavus and Gotthelf arrived at Mr. Childs' cottage in the horse-drawn photographic wagon. They were greeted by Childs who was on the front piazza with his friends, financier Anthony Drexel and the celebrated General Ulysses S. Grant.

The hard-working Pach brothers must have made a favorable impression upon Grant, Childs and Drexel. Perhaps something in their enthusiastic manner prompted the cigar-smoking General Grant to ask them why they didn't open up their own studio? The young men replied that they lacked the capital to do so. After Grant conferred with his affluent friends, Childs and Drexel each handed over five hundred dollars to the two young photographers. It was with this money that the Pach brothers were able to start their own photographic business in Long Branch.

At a time when some photographers were packing up their equipment and heading west to document the expanding frontier, the Pachs were opening their first studio in Long Branch. The "Pach's Photographic Gallery" was on the grounds of the huge oceanfront Continental Hotel. Their skylighted studio was in a remodeled former livery stable at the rear of the hotel's north wing, an excellent location providing the needed northern exposure so crucial for indoor portraiture.

The Pach brothers soon established another studio at the new resort of Ocean Grove, about nine miles south of Long Branch. In 1869, Ocean Grove began with a mere handful of tents and

Bathing Scene. Long Branch, 1870.

President Grant's Cottage. Long Branch, 1870.

President Grant and Family. Long Branch, 1872.

XIII

rapidly became the home of a huge Methodist Camp Meeting Association grounds. The Pach firm documented many hotels and boarding houses as well as tent life and beach front activities. Their first studio at Ocean Grove was located on Main Street, and a boardwalk establishment was later opened at the Ross Pavilion.

Although much of Pach Brothers' work was portraiture, they were especially proficient at landscape photography which was a difficult and challenging undertaking in those days. A book entitled *Album of Long Branch; A Series of Photographic Views with Letterpress Sketches* by J.H. Schenck was published in 1868. The now-rare volume was profusely illustrated with Pach views of Long Branch taken in 1867 and 1868. Each illustration was an original photographic print meticulously glued onto a single page by hand.

Like many other photographers, Pach Brothers also produced a variety of stereographic views. The stereograph is a pair of simultaneously exposed, almost identical, photographs mounted side by side which, when observed through the appropriate viewer (stereoscope), present a single picture in lifelike three dimensions. Stereographs were popular souvenirs in the pre-postcard era and the firm of Pach Brothers published nearly one thousand different Monmouth County, New Jersey, views between 1866 and 1885.

The favorable results of their first Long Branch studio prompted the Pach brothers to seek more than just a summer business. A year later they opened a studio in New York City at the Bowery on the third floor above a firehouse. The firm of Pach Brothers soon moved the New York operation to 858 Broadway where they were joined by an older brother, Oscar, who worked with them as a business manager. In 1878, Pach Brothers moved to 841 Broadway and in 1895, they relocated to a luxurious studio at 935 Broadway where they remained until 1910.

As the New York studio prospered, the Jersey Shore operation continued to flourish. When Ulysses S. Grant became President in 1869, he had his own Long Branch cottage which became known as "The Summer White House." Its presence increased the popularity of the resort. By the mid 1870's, a Pach studio was opened at the popular United States Hotel and during the 1880's a studio was opened at Brighton Avenue in the West End section of Long Branch. Pach's Lakewood photographic business on Clifton Avenue made its debut in 1896.

1868.

1874.

Pach photographers were taking pictures at Harvard, Yale, Princeton, and many other universities and colleges. With the support of President Ulysses S. Grant, Pach Brothers established a successful branch at West Point, Grant's alma mater. Gustavus Pach took pictures of the graduating class for over thirty years and was acquainted with many of the army officers.

In the late 1890's, at Princeton, New Jersey, G.W. Pach first met young George A.M. Morris. When Morris observed Pach taking photographs on the campus of Princeton University, he thought "photography looked easy enough to do and wanted to try it."

George Augustus Mengis Morris was born in Germany in 1879 but spent most of his childhood in an orphanage in Elizabeth, New Jersey. In his teens, he worked for a nurseryman until he decided to venture out on his own. It was then that he met G.W. Pach at Princeton University.

The handsome young Morris, reputed to be an excellent card player, did not have a permanent job until he asked Pach if he could work with him. Gustavus Pach took a liking to Morris and decided to give him a chance. George A. M. Morris began his photographic career at Pach's Lakewood studio in 1898.

When G.W. Pach opened the Lakewood business two years earlier, he found it to be a potentially profitable location. Lakewood, a fashionable "winter paradise," attracted many wealthy families at the turn of the century. Situated less than ten miles from Barnegat Bay and encircled by a magnificent pine forest, Lakewood was known for its relatively mild winters, healthy environment, and superb hotels.

From the very start of his career with G.W. Pach, George A.M. Morris was a success and customers soon began to request "that young boy" – referring to Morris. The charming and talented Morris learned the photographic trade quickly and established himself with influential clients including George Jay Gould, son of the infamous financier Jay Gould. For a decade, at the younger Gould's palatial estate at Lakewood (now Georgian Court College), Morris photographed George Jay Gould and his family. Eventually, Morris would even name his son George "Jay" Morris in honor of the Gould family.

The volume of Pach Brothers' work was so great that they needed to employ a number of capable photographers. Most of Pach Brothers, New York, business was portraiture and their excellent reputation attracted many celebrities. A booklet published by the New York firm describes their

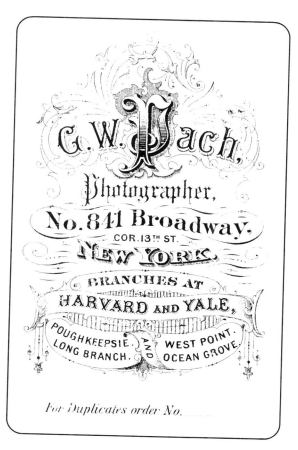

Ca. 1879.

George A. M. Morris.

work in the early twentieth century: "Pach cameras have captured a priceless record of the American scene. They have photographed Vanderbilt and Morgan, Longfellow and Twain, Thomas Edison and Irving Berlin, Lillian Russell and Maud Adams and thousands in between. They helped the New York Police Department set up its rogue's gallery, worked night and day photographing victims of the General Slocum excursion boat disaster (1,030 perished), and were star witnesses in the Metropolitan Museum-Cyprus scandal. And they photographed the presidents."

Theodore "Teddy" Roosevelt, the illustrious chief executive during most of *Those Innocent Years,* was photographed by Pach Brothers as a child in New York City and at every stage in his career – as a Harvard student, Rough Rider, and as President of the United States.

Alfred Meyer of Long Branch, a Pach photographer, took an often published family portrait of Teddy Roosevelt and his family at Sagamore Hill, their home in Oyster Bay, Long Island. According to the Long Branch Daily Record (August 13, 1903), "President Roosevelt pronounced the picture a gem, and highly complimented Pach Bros., and Mr. Meyer, the artist who so faithfully portrayed members of the family."

Alexander Pach was the son of Morris Pach, Gustavus and Gotthelf's eldest brother who operated a Red Bank, New Jersey, cigar business. Born in 1863 in Red Bank, Alex became permanently hearing-impaired at the age of seventeen. He had a successful career as a photographer with his uncles' firm, working at various branches and at the New York studio until his death in 1938.

G.W. Pach had become increasingly ill for a year and died of cancer in 1904. He was survived by his wife, Tillie; two sons, Jerome, 16 and Oscar, 14; and a daughter Minna, nicknamed "Billie," age 11. The family maintained a residence in Lakewood in the winter and one at Long Branch during the summer.

After G.W. Pach's death. George A.M. Morris carried on the New Jersey business. The Central Railroad of New Jersey was one of the large accounts. Morris took hundreds of photographs for the railroad's advertising brochures and booklets and also documented accident sites for the legal department. Morrris and his wife, Bessie, had a son, George Jay, and a daughter, Florence.

Gotthelf Pach became chief of the New York firm in 1903 when his brother, Gustavus took over the Jersey Shore studios. Gotthelf had two sons; Walter, a noted art historian, and Alfred, a photog-

Actress Lillian Russell. Ca. 1907.
Pach Brothers, New York.

President Roosevelt and Family. 1903.

rapher who became head of the New York operation when Gotthelf died in 1925 at the age of seventy-three. At this time the firm was at 570 Fifth Avenue; however, in 1933, it moved to 642 Fifth Avenue.

Today (1993), the New York firm of Pach Brothers, "the nation's oldest photography studio," is run by Oscar White who began his career as a photographer with Pach Brothers in 1939. Alfred Pach Sr. died in 1949, and in 1950, his son, Alfred Pach Jr. and Oscar White became partners, each holding a half interest in the business that was then located on East Fifty-seventh Street. In 1966, Alfred Pach Jr. sold his interest to Oscar White who then became the sole owner and president of the firm.

In 1967, Pach Brothers moved to its present location, 16 East Fifty-third Street. There, Oscar White carries on the Pach standards of excellence and continues the tradition of outstanding portraiture. He has photographed four U.S. Presidents and many other well-known personalities.

George A.M. Morris was instrumental in forming a New York corporation called Pach Photographer, Inc. in 1913, but that endeavor lasted for less than five years. As the former Pach firm that Morris operated at the Jersey Shore had ceased to exist by this time, Morris decided to work under his own name.

George Jay Morris, the son of George A.M. Morris, became a photographer, too. Father and son worked together for a short time, but this partnership ended as young George pursued a separate and successful career in industrial and advertising photography. George A.M. Morris continued to work for many years as an independent photographer. He died in 1948 in Long Branch. George Jay cared deeply about preserving his father's work and the "Pach Collection," for future generations.

The legacy of the Pach photographers at the Jersey Shore during *Those Innocent Years* lives on in this book. These black and white images need no artificial coloration – the vivid hues of flags and of flower-bedecked automobiles are evident. The rousing sound of a brass band, the steamy aroma of a clambake, the texture of ivory lace, and the taste of a chocolate eclair – such sensations can be perceived in this collection.

The success of the Pach photographers lies not only in their technical knowledge and artistic ability; but in the fact that, through their photographs, a viewer can truly experience the joy of *Those Innocent Years*.

Pach Studio, 935 Broadway, New York. 1896.

George Jay Morris. 1909.

G.W. Pach
LAKEWOOD AND
LONG BRANCH, N. J. (WEST END)
PORTRAITURE

PACH BROS.,
Photographists,
OCEAN GROVE & LONG BRANCH,
N. J.

15

THE MONITOR REGISTER.

YEAR 1899 DATE Month	Day	No. of Negative.	NAME	ADDRESS	Proof Sent / Ret.	No. and Style Ordered	Amount Paid	Amount Due	Whole Amount
Jan.	18	907	Gould dining room			14 X 17			
"	"	908	" Paintings			8 X 10			
"	"	909	" Miniatures						
"	"	910	Bourne Harold	Laurel in Pines		12 Imp	10	10	10
"	"	911	" Marjorie	" "		" "	10	10	10
"	"	912	The Hunt & Hounds			8 X 10			
"	"	913	Start of the Hunt			8 X 10			
"	"	914	Rosengarten Group	Lakewood Hotel 337 State St. Brooklyn		12 Cards	9	3 Imp 6 Cards	9
"	"	915	Kingdon Mrs.			28 Imp.		56	In
"	"	916	Kingsley Baby			12 Imp.	19	19	Pd N.Y.
"	"	917	Bryant Mrs. E.J. Wilson			6 Imp	6	6	Pd.
"	"	918	Kingsley Mr. & Baby			6	7	7	Pd. N.Y.
"	"	919	Kingsley Mrs.						
"	"	920	Golf Club			8 X 10			
"	"	921	Pine Park	Stock		14 X 17		Stock	
"	"	922	Blumenthal Mrs.			Imp			
"	"	923	Blumenthal Mr. Dining	54 W. 88 St.		6	6	6	Phila N.Y.
"	"	924	Garrett Mrs. & gp & horses	Mrs. J.J. Hegeman 1406 Pine St Phila		8 X 10	57	57	51
"	"	925	Perkins Mrs	111 Summer St. Boston, Mass.		11/14	16	16	16
"	"	926	Colt James W.			Imp		9	9
"	"	927	Colt Sylvia			"		9	9
"	"	928	Wilson Mr. E.J.			6		Pd in al

G. W. PACH,
PORTRAITURE,
LAKEWOOD AND LONG BRANCH,
NEW JERSEY.

G. W. PACH
PORTRAITURE
West End and Lakewood
N. J.

CHAPTER ONE

Portraits – formal and informal

In the early days of photography, it was the superior artistic ability of the individual behind the camera and not the camera itself, that was ultimately responsible for producing excellent portraits. Although there were many technological advances in photography by the beginning of the twentieth century, talented professional photographers still had to plan carefully and work diligently to create impressive images of their clients.

Amateur photography was a popular pastime during *Those Innocent Years.* Snapshots taken with simple box cameras, however, were not of sufficient quality for those special occasions and all-important portraits. Weddings, anniversaries, social gatherings, professional and fraternal organizations were all subjects for the portrait camera. Just as professional photographers are usually employed for milestone events in modern times, at the turn of the century, people relied upon able professionals to produce photographs of exceptional quality.

A good portrait artist needs to understand and capture the unique personality of an individual or the varying moods of a group. This also involves the photographer's ability to choose an appropriate background and put his subjects at ease. Outdoors or in the studio, the Pach photographers were masters of the art of portraiture. Lighting is obviously a critical factor to any portrait. At first, photographers relied on skylighted studios with a good northern exposure for their indoor portraits. By the time these Pach photographs were taken, flash powder and artificial light sources were being perfected. Photographers, however, were still using natural light for most of their indoor work.

The pictures in this chapter are representative of both formal and informal portraits – individual, family, or group – taken by G.W. Pach or George A.M. Morris. While these photographers took indoor portraits at the Long Branch and Lakewood studios, much of their business was also conducted outdoors. Pach and Morris and their associates depicted year-round residents as well as carefree visitors and "cottagers" including many celebrities from New York and Philadelphia. These clear images give a feeling of the devotion people had for their extended families, and pride in being members of civic and social groups.

Personal possessions and clothing were often influential factors in the portraits. Hats were popular and of importance to the people during this period. A mark of elegance or a statement of fashion, a woman's colossal ostrich plume hat or a man's sporty new straw boater would become the focal point of a portrait. Children were depicted with their favorite toy or a studio prop provided by the photographer. The toy, perhaps a doll or a stuffed animal, served a dual purpose – it added interest to the picture and also helped to keep an active child still. Children were frequently photographed in their favorite wagons and carts pulled by pet goats or ponies.

Those Innocent Years was a period of great demand for portraits of all subjects and occasions. A formal gift or a desirable keepsake, they were quite affordable and could preserve happy memories for years to come. G.W. Pach and George A.M. Morris produced thousands of appealing images, long forgotten, that now can be viewed not only for pleasure but for their historic significance.

With concentration and a touch of pride, Master Kauffman appears anxious to pedal his high-wheeled car, "Rocket."

Bk5481

Long Branch. 1908.

3

Bathed in soft sunlight, the image of this Seligman group
is a pleasant remembrance of times past.

As2029   Long Branch. 1903.

An engaging photograph of members of the Larrabee family is enhanced by the miniature horse cart, one of many props in the Pach studio.

Ml2221b

Lakewood. December 12, 1901.

*Two stern-faced uniformed "nannies" look directly at the camera
as two serious Guggenheimer children gaze at another point of interest.*

Bg1244b

Long Branch. 1902.

This exceptional portrait of Mrs. Curtis and her son highlights their stylish linen apparel.
The young boy in his sailor suit and his mother in a chic double-breasted
walking suit and holding an ivory-handled parasol represent the elegance of the era.

Bc5748

West End. 1908.

*Master Alfred Woehr appears to be scolding a naughty goat
in this amusing study. Or is he merely telling it to "stay?"*

Mw1044a   Lakewood. February 2, 1899.

*Minna Pach, daughter of G.W. Pach, entertains
her favorite dolls and cat with afternoon tea.*

Mp2236   Lakewood. February 1, 1899.

8

A difficult choice! The young Fisk boy must choose between riding his favorite pony or his goat-drawn "Favorite" wagon.

Af3703 & Af3704

West End. 1905.

9

With leather driving gloves and whip in hand, Mr. Savage proudly poses with his winning team in front of the New Monmouth Hotel.

Bs3997   Spring Lake. 1905.

*Just weeks before their marriage on April 29, 1911, young Jay Gould
and his fiancee, Anne Douglas Graham, were seen
in this handsome Mercedes at Georgian Court, his father's estate.*

XgMA100

Lakewood. April, 1911.

A softly-lit studio portrait captures "The C. E. Schauffler Child" contemplating a rubber toy and hints at the very essence of "Those Innocent Years."

Ms3527

Lakewood. March 17, 1905.

*A huge ostrich feather hat and an exquisite brocade dress
enhance the beauty of Miss D. Randolph.*

Ar4988   Long Branch. 1906.

*Lacking even a hint of a smile, Miss D. Fisk is photographed
in a fashionable lace dress and stylish feathered hat.*

Af4164   Long Branch. 1906.

14

Miss Tamire Pannaci, Queen of the 1911 Gala Long Branch Carnival,
was described by one New York newspaper as "…not only glowing
beauty but carriage and grace, and wears her gowns and hats
in a manner that suggests the Fifth Avenue type."
Governor Woodrow Wilson reviewed many of the festivities
which drew over 100,000 spectators by closing day.

Bp4526

Long Branch. July, 1911.

Posing for a photograph at their annual outing, the Merchant Tailors group represents a subtle fashion statement of the period.

In a humorous vein, two photographs were taken of "the Johnson Group." In one view the women are seated while in this, the second view, the men are seated.

Wardell's Port-au-Peck Hotel. 1908.

Gj493

A matchless outdoor portrait of George Jay Gould and his wife, Edith, and their children at Georgian Court. Gould holds the hand of his daughter, Vivien, and little Edith stands in front of her mother. Arms folded, young George is seated at right. Standing in the rear

G.W.PACH LAKEWOOD, N.J.
COPYRIGHT 1905

With great attention to detail, these beautifully-designed dresses and stylish hats add much to this formal Woerz family portrait.

Rumson. 1908.

Cw356

This Bettina Pannaci-Herbert Booth wedding portrait includes maid of honor, Tamire Pannaci, sister of the bride, and parents, Mr. and Mrs. G. Pannaci, at right. Also, Mrs. Emma Moss, front row left, and her two sons; S. D. Moss, extreme left, and G. H. Moss Sr., extreme right, rear.

Several generations of the Niles family sit for this pleasing picture at a special reunion.

Monmouth Beach. 1907.

Cn267

*Portly John A. McCall gazes intently at the youngest member
of the "McCall Group." After spending a few summers
at Allenhurst, the McCalls moved into their new home,
"Shadow Lawn," in West Long Branch.*

Am4159

Allenhurst. 1902.

*In a peaceful and quiet atmosphere, Mr. and Mrs. A. H. Calef relax
in the screened porch privacy of their large oceanfront home.*

Ac2499

North Beach, Sea Bright. 1903.

*The pleasure of the moment is preserved in this charming portrait
of three generations of the Stockton family.*

As2812

Possibly Long Branch. 1904.

*The long-time proprietor of Price's Hotel at Pleasure Bay,
Edward Hartshorne Price, and a faithful canine friend
are pictured in a quiet outdoor setting.*

Ap2289   Long Branch. 1904.

Samuel L. Clemens, the incomparable Mark Twain, is photographed on the occasion of a luncheon given for his friend and fellow author William Dean Howells. On the right is Dorothy Harvey, a daughter of Deal resident Colonel George Harvey, editor-in-chief of Harper & Brothers.

At4637

Lakewood. 1907.

At the luncheon given for Howells, a formidable "literary group" assembled for this Pach portrait
which has since appeared in many books including an edition of Mark Twain's autobiography.
From left to right are Howells, Twain, Harvey, H. M. Alden (editor of Harpers for over fifty years),
David M. Munro and M. W. Hazeltine, also editors associated with Harper and Brothers.

Ah4433   Lakewood. 1907.

Monmouth Beach, N. J. Summer Cottages.

OCEAN AVENUE, LONG BRANCH, N. J.

100258

Beach and Bluff, Long Branch, N. J.

CHAPTER TWO

The Changing Scene

The landscape all around us can be compared to the staging of a lavish theatrical production with constant changes of scenery. At the Jersey Shore, man and nature have jointly contributed to these changing scenes. This ongoing process is not always perceived until that which was changed has become but a memory.

Two views of the northern portion of Sea Bright taken in 1910 clearly show subtle but major changes to that area. One photograph shows the almost forgotten location of the Central Railroad tracks paralleling Ocean Avenue while another graphically depicts one of the less than protective early seawalls.

Much of the charm of the Jersey Shore was (and still is) found in the magnificent architectural treasures that were the great estates and summer homes of the wealthy. A few of these great homes have been selected for their obvious grandeur, difference in design and, importantly, for what they represented in the changing lifestyle at the Jersey Shore.

Fine examples of the varied architectural endeavors of the period are the former E.G.W. Woerz home and neighboring "Rohallion," the original estate of Edward Dean Adams. Located in Rumson, both have been structurally modified since they were first built. Many of the impressive homes that contributed to the architectural reputation of the Jersey shore are now long gone. Two particularly significant examples in this category were John A. McCall's in Long Branch and Martin Maloney's estate in Spring Lake.

Situated precariously close to the ocean, two of the dozens of grand and spacious summer Sea Bright "cottages" are only photographic memories. An interior view offers some idea of the elegance of one of these summer residences. Through the years, a number of large beach front homes in both Sea Bright and Monmouth Beach were destroyed by fire and storm. Of them all, only two homes still survive in their original location. A few others have survived natural disasters having been moved to less vulnerable locations years ago.

Time goes hand in hand with change. Condominiums and beach clubs now exist where once a cottage colony enjoyed a summer sunrise and cool ocean breezes at Monmouth Beach. At Long Branch, a modern hotel overlooks a bluff and ocean from a site long identified with much of the early history of this well known Victorian "watering place."

Wide boardwalks and even wider beaches are no more. Again, nature contributed to those changes. Most of the grand hotels that catered to more than one generation are long-forgotten. Boardwalk bandstands with stirring summer programs by Sousa and Pryor are obviously gone. Even the thoughts of a moonlit promenade by the sea or of a peaceful Sunday afternoon ride in a weathered rowboat are part of the past – but tastes change, too.

The open land of North Asbury Park soon became fully developed. While the tranquil scene at the Avon Casino changed but little, Buhler's boat basin, on the other hand, became part of the present site of the huge Belmar Marina. In Spring Lake, a number of homes now cover the estate where once a single summer mansion stood. Change has taken place at the Jersey Shore. It no is longer purely a summer playground as most of the area has developed into a thriving year round place in which to live.

A solitary pony cart at the corner of Ward Avenue and Rumson Road reflects the tranquility of the period. Both the Haddon house (built in 1889 and designed by Sidney Stratton) and the larger home, at right, (built in 1890, and designed by Stratton & Ellingwood) were later bought by Bernon S. Prentice. The major portion of the property eventually became the site of Holy Cross School and Convent.

Xc300

Rumson. 1903.

A bright summer sun highlights the intricate pattern of wood shingles of E. G. Woerz's residence. Built in 1884 for John D. Ewell, it was moved in 1890 from Ward Avenue to the southeast corner of Navesink Avenue and Rumson Road. Having survived a fire in later years, it now stands in a dramatically remodeled state.

A landscape view of "Rohallion," the vast estate of financier Edward Dean Adams. It was originally designed by Stanford White and built in 1887-88. Nathan Barrett was the noted landscape architect.

A5

Rumson. 1903.

This view of North Beach clearly shows the Central Railroad of New Jersey's right-of-way running parallel between Ocean Avenue and the protective seawall (off camera) on the right.

Taken at a different angle, this picture graphically illustrates the seawall only as a minor deterrent against the potential forces of nature.

Sea Bright. May, 1912.

CS9001

Facing the ocean and situated east of the railroad tracks, the vulnerable oceanfront location of A. H. Calef's North Beach residence (designed by Daniel W. Willard and built in 1882) was typical of more than a dozen summer cottages in the area.

The ocean side of the Calef estate included a boardwalk, and a series of protective bulkheads. They were newly built in 1892 to replace ones washed away by a prior storm. Having also lost his lawn at that time, Calef had his residence moved back about forty feet from the ocean. Mrs. Calef is seen quietly reading in this peaceful early morning setting.

C44b

Sea Bright. 1903.

West of the main house – beyond the railroad tracks and Ocean Avenue – was Calef's stable. Pleasantly situated, its location afforded a sweeping view of nearby Rumson estates across the Shrewsbury River.

On Ocean Avenue, south of the Peninsula Hotel (just off camera at left), are more handsome oceanfront residences of Sea Bright's prestigious summer cottage colony.

Sea Bright. 1903.

C294b

Still further south on Ocean Avenue, in the Low Moor section of Sea Bright, and located dangerously close to the ocean, is William Nelson Cromwell's magnificent summer estate.

This interior view of the main hall, provides a glimpse of the elegance of the Cromwell home.

Sea Bright. 1903.

C50b

Situated at the water's edge, Cromwell's residence, like others in the area, often felt the effects of a storm-driven ocean. Through the years many homes were severely damaged or even washed out to sea. A few were fortunately moved to safer locations. In 1947, Cromwell's former home was totally destroyed by fire.

Photographed from Cromwell's residence, this breathtaking view of his stable captures the beauty of open space along the South Shrewsbury River. With Rumson in the distance, a solitary paddlewheel steamer, the LITTLE SILVER, *heads for Pleasure Bay, Long Branch. The Central Railroad tracks can be seen behind the stable.*

C50d

Sea Bright. 1903.

Looking north and east along Ocean Avenue from Valentine Street, Monmouth Beach, this view provides a glimpse of another group of oceanfront cottages. Banker George F. Baker's residence, "Seaverge," (built ca. 1884 by Bruce Price) is at the extreme right.

Located in Ocean Park at the corner of Broadway and Ocean Avenue, remodeled a few times and known as the Casino Annex and the Ocean Villa, this building was a center of entertainment for a number of years. The renowned Carlisle (Pa.) Indian Band, a major shore attraction, performed many concerts before enormous crowds at this location.

Long Branch. 1905.

Co3449

"Shadow Lawn" was built in 1903 for John A. McCall, president of the New York Life Insurance Co., by architect Henry Edward Cregier. McCall died in 1905, and title to the property subsequently changed hands five times until it was purchased in 1909 by Joseph B. Greenhut. Used as a summer White House by Woodrow Wilson in 1916, "Shadow Lawn" was purchased by Hubert T. Parsons, president of F. W. Woolworth Company in 1918. After this magnificent home was destroyed by fire in 1927, it was replaced by an $8,000,000 mansion designed by Horace Trumbauer and is now part of Monmouth College.

Henry E. Creiger's attention to detail is evident in this photograph of John A. McCall's beautifully designed Coach House and Stable.

Cmc219

West Long Branch. 1904.

*This undeveloped portion of North Asbury Park is an unusual scene
– particularly when observed from the Hotel Loch Arbour, across Deal Lake.*

Aax301   Asbury Park. 1905.

Near the end of the season, the crowds on the beach are still taking advantage
of another beautiful day at the shore. The hotels, the wide boardwalk
with a variety of amusements and the Arcade in the distance,
were part of the attraction of this popular resort.

Aa3637   Asbury Park. September 1, 1905.

An open-air boardwalk concert given by Arthur Pryor's Band holds the attention of the seated audience as well as those people in the passing autombiles and carriages.

Xa206

Asbury Park. 1906.

To the far right of the on-going band concert, many other attentive listeners
prefer to sit in the shade of the attractive Asbury Park Casino.

Xa207

Asbury Park. 1906.

*Even late in the season, a breezy but sunny few hours on the beach
of the popular Avon Casino were considered a rewarding adventure.*

Xa3822   Avon-by-the-Sea. September. 1905.

Photographed for a Central Railroad of New Jersey advertisement,
this pleasant Shark River scene of Buhler's Sail and Rowboat Pavilion
is now replaced by the busy Belmar Marina.

Mb3653

Belmar. September 1, 1905.

This impressive residence, "Ballingarry," was designed by Horace Trumbauer and built in 1897 for Martin Maloney, a member of the Wall Street community. Mr. Maloney can be seen reading a newspaper on his front porch. He later gave St. Catharine's Church, also designed by Trumbauer, in memory of a deceased daughter.

In 1896, ground was broken in Lakewood for financier George Jay Gould's magnificent country estate, Georgian Court. Seen here in the midst of a surrounding pine forest is an overall landscape view of the two-hundred-acre site. Designed by architect Bruce Price and first occupied in 1897, the fifty-room mansion is now part of Georgian Court College.

Mg200x

Lakewood. 1905.

At the sea-shore I was the centre of attraction.

CHAPTER THREE

Leisure Time Activities

The New Jersey Shore with its ever-changing beaches and moody ocean has always been one of the State's major attractions. More than a century ago, the spirit of the sparkling surf, sunlit sand and activities of joyful summer visitors were captured by many of America's foremost artists including Winslow Homer.

Although ocean bathing or promenading on the bluff or boardwalk were always popular, other recreational opportunities gradually became available at the shore. During the first decade of the twentieth century, horse shows, dog shows, society carnivals and circuses, baby parades, automobile parades and automobile races and even air shows attracted thousands of delighted visitors.

There were also local theaters showing both stage plays direct from New York as well as popular acts from the various vaudeville circuits. Band concerts by the sea were well attended events. John Philip Sousa, Arthur Pryor and Pennsylvania's entertaining Carlisle Indian School Band were all favorites for many years at the Jersey Shore.

Spectator or participant, there was ample opportunity to be involved in recreational golf, baseball, football, bowling or bicycling. The League of American Wheelmen did much to promote interest in the latter at the shore. Tennis, croquet and bicycling were particular sports enjoyed by both sexes.

Baseball and boxing were generally considered America's favorite spectator sports and, by the turn of the century, entrepreneurs made large sums of money from organizing teams and promoting matches. Surprisingly, from the 1890's through 1917, many professional and semi-professional baseball teams played in Asbury Park and Long Branch. Big league games (Long Branch vs. the New York Yankees!) were often played in West End's Hollywood Horse Show Grounds.

Polo, a sport of the privileged few, had an avid following as did "riding to the hounds." Perhaps the most elite sport of all was practiced by the exclusive Coaching Club. The ultimate goal of its members was to own and drive a public coach that carried paying passengers between two points of departure on a fixed schedule. In 1903, flamboyant member James H. Hyde accomplished that by driving his coach between Lakewood, New Jersey, and New York City.

Though an obvious necessity, eating was also an enjoyable recreational activity that appealed to everyone. Lavish meals, a holdover from the earlier Victorian era, were still served in luxurious hotels and restaurants and, of course, in private homes. But, it was the less formal and more relaxed style of dining that had the greatest appeal. Typically, the festive and filling "shore dinner" was the attraction and climax of lighthearted social and business outings. On the banks of the Shrewsbury River, mouth-watering clambakes were held in high esteem by some groups; while in nearby shady groves, picnics delighted smaller family gatherings.

Ball game or horse show, formal dinner or picnic, all were celebrations of life that reflected the growing social and economic importance of leisure time.

Against a studio backdrop and with glove, bat and baseball, J. C. Parrish Jr. poses in a uniform of America's most popular sport.

Mp755d Lakewood. May 21, 1898.

Two years later, Kingdon Gould and brother Jay, young polo enthusiasts, sit for this casual portrait in the same Pach Studio.

Mg1640a Lakewood. June 9, 1900.

William Schauffler models the latest protective gear for an ice hockey player.

Xs5151a Lakewood. 1904.

The Converse boys, looking for a game of croquet, also found themselves in the familiar surroundings of Pach's Studio.

Mc2064a Lakewood. May 16, 1901.

Sportsman James H. Hyde's coach "Liberty" prepares to leave Lakewood's Laurel-in-the-Pines for New York City's fashionable Holland House. The nine-and-a-half-hour trip required ten changes of horses! Returning to Lakewood on the following day, amateur Coachman Hyde continued to maintain this incredible schedule for six weeks.

In front of Sea Bright's Pannaci Hotel, Alfred G. Vanderbilt and others prepare for the annual six mile road race along Ocean Avenue to the Hollywood Horseshow Grounds at West End. In 1905, Vanderbilt won this race in a time of twenty-six minutes.

Sea Bright. 1907.

Cv349

*Indian clubs, dumbbells, boxing gloves, a bicycle and a bottle of beer
are indicative of the varied interests of the Darlington Sporting Club members.*

Ad1523   Darlington, (Deal Beach). 1900.

*More than this slate was used to tally scores. On the wall is written
"A.R.Fisk Jan 14th. '98 203." Two additional impressive scores
(300 and 298) were recorded on March and April of 1896.*

Mb689 - flash   Lakewood. March 28, 1898.

*With the ocean in the distance, this late afternoon baseball game holds
the attention of all the spectators. The vehicle at the extreme
right is Pach's ever-present Photographic Wagon.*

Aa2480   Allenhurst Baseball Field. 1904.

Tough and formidable, this Long Branch football team is ready for any challenge.

Al2717

Long Branch. 1905.

*Two youthful caddies keep a watchful eye on the photographer
while the players keep an eye on the ball.*

Mg1491a

Lakewood. February 24, 1900.

Attracted by this particular game at the Norwood Club, passersby in carriages stop and, like the seated spectators, continue to watch an exciting mid-day tennis match played under a sweltering summer sun.

An2223

West Long Branch. 1904.

Smiling Hollywood Charity Amateur Circus Clowns, ready to join others in a major fund-raising event for Monmouth Memorial Hospital (now Monmouth Medical Center), wave from this uncommon Stoddard-Dayton touring car.

Bh4288p

West End. 1909.

Featured in twenty stage productions between 1893 and 1910, attractive musical comedy star Adele Ritchie (seated on bicycle) and friend appear amused as they eye their serious male companion.

Ar2361

Long Branch. 1904.

*Publisher Peter F. Collier and son Robert (right) pose for the camera
before the start of another famous Collier Hunt.*

Mc3196a

Lakewood. April 11, 1904.

"Beadleston's English Bull and Pup." This charming photo of a pipe-smoking gentleman
and his two contented show dogs, once seen, will long be remembered.

Xb2491

West End. 1911.

One of the enjoyable attractions at Asbury Park was the Boardwalk. The mid-day stroll past the Seventh Avenue Pavilion was a daily social event.

Xa200

Asbury Park. 1905.

Clad in wool bathing suits, these smiling Octagon Hotel bathers playfully pose for their photograph. In the background is the Hotel's Restaurant Pier.

Ao2584

Sea Bright. 1904.

In the Shrewsbury River, opposite the Highlands of Navesink and the historic Twin Lights, the houseboat ELECTRA quietly rides at anchor.

Highland Beach. 1905.

The MARY EMMA hard aground, the result of a sudden storm the day before, attracts a crowd of young onlookers. Offshore commercial pound nets are visible in the distance.

Sea Bright-Long Branch area. 1906.

"America's Greatest Aviation Meet," held at Interlaken Field, featured the Wright Brothers newest aeroplane and pioneer aviators Brookins, Hoxsey and Coffyn. New altitude records (barely over 500 feet) were set daily by these pilots as they flew over the field to the cheers of excited spectators.

Ba4702a, b, c.

Asbury Park. Mid-August, 1910.

Elkwood Park (the site of present day Monmouth Park Race Track) hosted many events including trotting races, automobile races and even clay pigeon shooting.

Be4047

Oceanport. 1907.

The Hollywood Horse Show Grounds, for over two decades, held the most prestigious outdoor horse show in America. Attended by leaders of society, Horse Show Week included a major carnival, parades, teas, receptions, dances and other social affairs.

Bh4656

West End. 1909.

Held at the Hollywood Hotel, this Stern family dinner must have been for a very special occasion. The two heart-shaped boxes might indicate an anniversary or engagement party.

"Mrs. P. Rhinelander's Dinner." Beneath the flag-draped ceiling and windows, could the table decorations of a small canon, flags, drums, and a patriotic picture in front of everyone suggest a 4th of July birthday celebration?

Long Branch?. 1904.

Cr286 - flash

At this shady picnic grove, the late afternoon sun manages
to highlight the smiling faces of the McCue family clambake.

Bm4192

Pleasure Bay. 1907.

A costume party given at Georgian Court by George Jay Gould (in formal Scottish attire, lower right)
proved to be less than an exciting affair. The guests were attended to by a dozen servants.

Over hot coals and covered by a tarpaulin, bushels of local clams are steamed in a bed of seaweed along with ears of Jersey corn and chicken - all part of a tasty Shore Dinner.

On the banks of the busy South Shrewsbury River, with Patten Line steamboats in the distance, waiters stand by the outdoor table ready to serve platters of clams at an on-going dinner party inside Wardell's restaurant.

Wardell's. Port-Au-Peck. 1907.

Cc61

Members of the Crab Club, a social group, pose for their annual after-dinner photograph. The club "comedian" holds up last year's picture, which shows him holding up the previous year's photo. Champagne is the drink of the day.

Inside Wardell's Restaurant one can see the remains of the last course of the Crab Club's Annual Clam Bake Dinner - watermelon. The twenty-eight quart bottles of Mumm Champagne and one bottle of beer on the table helped make this a festive occasion!

Cc4923

Wardell's. Port-Au-Peck. 1907.

CHAPTER FOUR

The Business Community

The Jersey Shore, traditionally, "came alive" during the summer months. "Cottagers" returned for the season, hotels reopened, and on a daily basis, thousands of people left the uncomfortable cities for a brief but exhilarating moment by the sea.

It is quite evident that there was a remarkable difference between the first decade of the Twentieth Century and the last decade of the Nineteenth Century. There was a revival, a renaissance of activity, at the Jersey Shore.

Affluent times and expanding building programs produced a vibrant interest in the area. Newer methods of communication, transportation and improved accommodations also contributed to this awakening. Homes and hotels now had electricity and telephones. With all the latest amenities, hotels were booked for the season. There were more attractions and there was more freedom to enjoy newfound leisure time in *Those Innocent Years.*

Local businesses of every description usually supported the wide-ranging needs of most of the shore communities. Many commercial enterprises, often family owned for more than one generation, served the general public on a year round basis. Blacksmiths and carriage makers still enjoyed a viable business although garages were assuming a more important role in this changing society. For even in commerce, the automobile would soon overtake the horse.

While obviously looking forward to the summer population growth, Finley's Belmar Central Market, on the other hand, was open all year round. The Christmas Holiday butcher shop display was typical for the season. Here are offered a variety of hams from Ferris of New York, from Kingan and from Swift & Company. Turkeys, chickens, legs of lamb, sides of bacon and an incredible array of standing rib roasts almost detract from the blue-ribboned half-skinned steer.

Founded in New York in 1840, long respected Park & Tilford brought from the city a sophisticated world of imported teas, coffees, fancy groceries, liquors, vintage wines and prized cigars from Havana and Key West.

Cella's Brighton Avenue Market, a branch of their New York store, displayed a variety of the choicest fresh fruits and vegetables available. Next door was another fine New York City grocery firm – Acker, Merrall and Condit.

A few doors away, Maison Francaise, a newly formed first-class catering establishment, supplied fresh soups, consommes, salads, entrees, and roasts as well as their own ice cream and pastries. Imported delicacies included canned mushrooms, anchovies, and jars of brandied peaches, and preserved chestnuts in syrup.

On nearby Ocean Avenue, Huyler's, another popular favorite from New York, tempted everyone with their fine selection of candies.

Prestigious New York firms (mostly specialty food stores and fine grocers) wisely continued to service their out-of-town summer customers by opening branch stores at the shore. Busy and exciting Long Branch in particular, after more than a century, was still a premier summer resort. West End's Brighton Avenue, in turn, was the gourmet marketplace of the Jersey Shore.

The Casino, formerly known as Johnson's Club House and located next to Phil Daly's old Pennsylvania Club, was a restaurant noted for its fine cusine. In 1902 it was managed by Rudolph Busse (of New York's Holland House) and by E. Witte (of Sherry's). With enlarged dining facilities and later known as the West End Shore Club, the restaurant's excellent reputation still attracted a loyal following in 1910.

Cw563b

Ocean Avenue, West End. 1910.

Uniformed Long Branch Letter Carriers sternly eye the camera for their official photograph.

Al2837

Long Branch. 1903.

Although primarily blacksmiths, Charles and Israel Reid were also excellent carriage builders. Their business establishment was located at 8 North Broadway.

Mr3335

Long Branch. June 14, 1902.

*A. Percy Sherman's (Meat) Market rig won the ten dollar first prize
at the 3rd Annual Rumson Horse Show.*

Ms3734   Rumson. July 7, 1905.

*Clancey's Farm Dairy Wagon (with horse "Billy") won third prize at the same event.
Clancey's is another firm that branched out from New York City to the Jersey Shore.*

Mc3736   Rumson. July 7, 1905.

Lakewood Farms, producers of "Fancy Farm Products," offered the finest grade of eggs, poultry, butter, vegetables and fruit. Their extensive farms were located in Vineland, Lakewood and Eatontown.

Al4720

Lincoln Avenue, Elberon. 1910.

A smiling Jerry Pach, son of G. W. Pach, drives the firm's Photographic Wagon past the old Monmouth Beach Casino. Pach's Wagon appears discreetly in a number of outdoor scenic views.

Ap2287

Monmouth Beach. 1904.

The New York firm of Acker, Merrall & Condit Company, grocers, with branches in Sea Bright, Red Bank and West End, displays its new electric delivery wagon.

Aa1192

West End. 1910.

Garages were kept busy with constant automotive problems. It is doubtful all problems were taken as lightly as this particular one. Involved in a severe collision, this Stearns car was in obvious need of more than tire repair.

Bs4627c

West End. 1909.

Flat tires, one of the most frustrating and recurring problems for early "automobilists,"
fortunately, could be quickly repaired. With his ready supply of rubber inner tubes,
dependable Mr. O'Connor saved many a pleasant automobile outing
from turning into a disappointing event.

Ao6266a & Ao6266b

West End. 1909.

Situated on Ocean Avenue, Morris C. Burns and Robert Tappin's Columbia Baths offered customers invigorating "hot and cold sea water baths, salt water plunge and surf bathing" as well as refreshing "Orange Phosphates, Ice Cream Sodas and assorted sparkling waters."

Ac1845

Long Branch. 1902.

Another noted firm from New York, Huyler's Ocean Avenue store, was noted for delicious ice cream, bon bons, fine chocolate and ice cold soda water.

Ah1556

West End. 1909.

Originally built as the Stetson House in 1867 and called "the dwelling place of the elite,"
the West End Hotel could accommodate eight hundred guests. Located at the corner
of Ocean and Brighton Avenues, it was torn down in 1906.

Aw3523

West End. 1902.

Cheerful waitresses gather outdoors on the steps of the Darlington Inn
for this rather informal portrait.

Ad1522   Darlington, (Deal Beach). 1900.

*"Wardell's Pleasure Bay Waiters." J. H. Wardell's well-known hotel was the scene
of many shore dinners and outdoor clambakes. For this photograph,
the staff paused from their busy routine.*

Bw3933

Port-au-Peck. 1905.

*Although the sound of their music can no longer be heard, at least Wardell's popular
and talented Port-au-Peck Musicians can be seen in this studio portrait.*

Bp4489

Port-au-Peck. 1909.

Nicholas West's "Green Gables" was another "clambake resort" of note. The small glass enclosed pavilions housed private dining facilities. "Green Gables" was also a favorite rendezvous for sailing parties.

North Pleasure Bay, July, 1902.

Cw367

The interior view of A. Finley's Central Market offers a Christmas Holiday display of choice meats and poultry. A most interesting item is the young prize-winning half-skinned steer atop the rear counter.

The local branch of Charles Higgins' Madison Avenue, New York, butcher shop and Walker's neighboring Columbia Restaurant were located in the middle of the business district at 119 Brighton Avenue, West End.

West End. 1911.

Ch479

Angelica Cella's Brighton Avenue fruit store before it was remodeled and enlarged.
Cella's, the neighboring bicycle store and Donnelly's Dairy were just a few
of the many New York businesses with branches located at the shore.
Summer visitors were loyal to their city merchants.

West End. 1901.

*Angelica Cella's impressive display of mid-summer fruits and vegetables. A variety
of fresh pears, plums, grapes, peaches, pineapples, cantelopes and watermelons
surrounds the celery, beets and turnips in the background. The doorway poster
advertises the Allenhurst-Deal annual Amateur Circus and Wild West
Show for the benefit of St. Mary's and St. Andrew's Churches.*

Bc3674

West End. August, 1905.

Leon Cottentin (sixth from left), who had a longtime association with Hoey's Hollywood Hotel and the West End Cottages, formed a partnership with M. Pirolle, an experienced french chef and pastry cook. Their Maison Francaise opened for business on June 15th, 1907.

In a Spartan kitchen, and under M. Pirolle's strict supervision, the staff prepared many tempting examples of fine French cuisine. Pirolle's directive "No Smoking Allowed in This Room"
— was, perhaps, ahead of its time.

West End. July 27, 1907.

Cc437b

Baskets of Pirolle's fresh brioche, displays of eclairs, fruit tarts, petits fours and a variety of cookies and chocolate treats often presented pleasant but difficult decisions.

Shelves of imported French delicacies, Spanish red pimentos and cans of Green Turtle Soup line another wall of Maison Francaise. The glass topped cabinet housed available tender roasts and smoked meats. Another speciality of the house – imported party decorations – added a lively touch to many gala affairs.

West End. July 27, 1907.

Cc437d

With five first-class stores in New York City, Park & Tilford, opened a business establishment at 47 Brighton Avenue on July 14, 1906. Catering to the tastes of the sophisticated summer "cottagers," Park & Tilford offered a variety of well-known imported delicacies.

Cp375b

West End. 1906.

112

Perhaps Park & Tilford's initialed stained glass window at the top of the stairs proclaimed the quality within. Shelves of desirable delicacies line the wall, while imported biscuits and jars of brandied cherries are displayed in stacks on the floor. Also visible are bottles of liqueurs, fine wines and vintage (1900) Champagnes.

West End. 1906.

Cp376

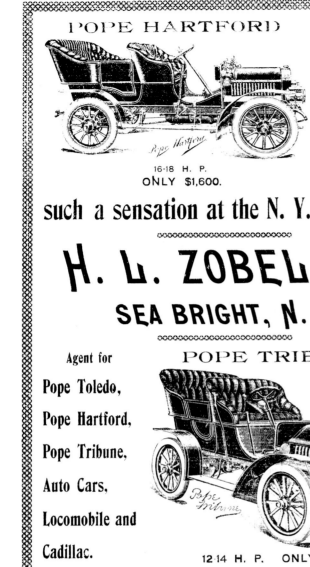

CHAPTER FIVE

The Automobile Comes of Age

As *Those Innocent Years* began, the automobile was no longer a mechanical curiosity. The exciting possibilities of the horseless carriage quickly seized the imagination of the American public. While there were only eight thousand registered passenger vehicles in the entire United States in 1900; by 1914, the total had soared to over a million and a half!

In the first decade, automobiles were powered by either electricity, steam or gasoline. Prices for American cars ranged from around three hundred to more than seven thousand dollars, yet most vehicles, still costly, sold for under twenty-five hundred dollars. Desirable, more expensive European cars were a sign of affluence. By 1901, Lakewood multi-millionaire George Jay Gould, for example, owned five popular French automobiles.

Some automobiles were affordable to the average person, but because of the high cost of upkeep and operation, motoring was considered a "sport" at this time. Necessary protective clothing – including tailored fur or leather winter coats, lighter dust coats ("dusters"), special hats, scarves, veils, goggles, and gloves – was another unavoidable expense. Muddy or dusty, the early rutted dirt roads made driving both a hazard and a challenge. However, by 1914 there were significant changes. Roads were being paved, Henry Ford was mass producing cars and overall automotive maintenance costs were declining.

The automobile contributed to the gaiety and excitement of *Those Innocent Years*. Dozens of songs were written about this remarkable machine during that time. "Love in an Automobile" (1899) was one of the earliest, while "In My Merry

Oldsmobile" (1905) was the most popular. Names were also a point of humor as FORD was often interpreted as meaning "Fix Or Repair Daily"; Evertt-Metzger-Flanders or E-M-F as "Every Mechanical Failure" and Ransom E. Olds' REO as "Runs Every Opportunity."

More than two thousand different makes of automobiles were manufactured in the United States during the first decades of the industry. Often producers of fine cars, many of these new companies ceased to exist within a few years because of financial difficulties or business mergers.

Just as horse-drawn carriages (Coaches, Phaetons, Pony Carts, Surreys, Turnouts, Victorias, Wagonettes, etc.) were designed for specific needs, so were automobiles. The mechanical vehicles readily evolved into a variety of styles including Broughams, Cabriolets, Limousines, Landaulets, Roadsters and Speedsters. Buyers who could afford more than one style of automobile did so for the same reasons they purchased a variety of carriages in the past. The jaunty little Runabout, the imposing seven passenger Touring Car or the formal Landaulet were each designed for a different purpose.

Delighted automobile owners often wanted to be photographed with their new vehicles just as they were photographed in previous years with their horses and carriages. In 1905, Charles C. Miller of Long Branch gladly displayed his diversified collection of six impressive vehicles for a Pach photographer. Other Jersey Shore owners were photographed with their new cars and the resulting pictures provide a glimpse of some rare and obscure examples of these vintage automobiles.

For many years automobile parades were popular and entertaining spectacles. One of Sea Bright's earlier parades of this kind took place soon after the dedication of the new Sea Bright-Rumson Bridge in 1901. Many of the participating vehicles were either electric or steam powered.

In 1905, Long Branch held its second annual week-long Automobile Carnival. Parades, shows and even auto races at nearby Elkwood Park thrilled enthusiastic spectators. Vehicles decorated with colorful flowers came from Spring Lake and surrounding towns to join others in competition for handsome silver trophies awarded for originality of design.

The first Long Branch Baby Parade was part of a two-day Carnival along the bluff and boardwalk in 1909. A great success (and held for a number of years thereafter), the events of the closing day included a spectacular automobile parade witnessed by seventy-five thousand people. Shaped like a large swan, one vehicle was covered with four thousand flowers consisting of heliotropes and purple and lilac hydrangeas. Expenses were of little consideration as floral decorations for four other cars cost twenty-five hundred dollars. While many automobiles were covered with flowers and flags, some innovative owners transformed their cars into boats and even aeroplanes!

Although the familiar and dependable horse and carriage remained in contention for a few more decades, the automobile – an exciting and more sophisticated means of transportation – soon became a part of the American Dream.

The late afternoon train had stopped at the Sea Bright Station just moments before this picture was taken. With no automobiles yet to be seen, weary commuters from New York now head for home in horse-drawn carriages. At the far right, a few visitors walk towards the nearest hotel.

Cs294a   Sea Bright. 1900.

*Four-year-old George Jay Gould Jr. and "Engineer" Blumet
are photographed in this new French De Dion-Bouton
Gasoline Quadricycle on the grounds of Georgian Court.*

Mg1750   Lakewood. December 11, 1900.

*Posed in front of Georgian Court's Casino, "Engineer" Blumet
and young George are seated in George Jay Gould's
impressive French Panhard-Levassor.*

Mg1748   Lakewood. December 11, 1900.

George Jay Gould's children (Kingdon and Marjorie on the left and Jay and Vivien on the right) display their personal De Dion-Boutons. In his own miniature electric auto, George, Jr. copies the pose of the "Engineer" seated behind the steering wheel of his father's Panhard-Levassor. Because of his attire, young George is often mis-identified as his younger sister Edith. Edith was only five months old at this time.

Lakewood. January 17, 1902.

*In a tastefully decorated De Dion-Bouton and with Rumson and the Highland Hills
in the background, the Martin group (riding in M. F. Warburg's car)
await the start of an exciting parade.*

Bw3871

Sea Bright. 1901.

*Next in line, President of the First National Bank of Sea Bright and proprietor
of the Octagon Hotel, George M. Sandt and companion
arrive in this flower-decorated vehicle.*

Bs3967

Sea Bright. 1901.

*Mr. Cook, in a popular Waverly Electric, keeps his eyes on the traffic ahead
as more vehicles arrive. Edward Dean Adams and other participants
move into position in the rear as the parade is about to begin.*

Bc3671

Sea Bright. 1901.

*Rumsonite Edward Dean Adams rides past the Sea Bright Railroad Station
and joins the rest of the assembled "automobilists."*

Aa4805

Sea Bright. 1901.

Six-year-old George Jay Gould, Jr. and the doll-like "Mackay girl" are photographed in George's own electric auto, a Christmas gift from his father.

Mg2437c

Lakewood. April 13, 1902.

George veers off the path as the young couple tour the Gould estate.

Mg2437h

Lakewood. April 13, 1902.

122

Mrs. G. W. Pach and family members prepare for a sunny but cool afternoon drive. Lake Carasaljo is in the background.

Mp3009   Lakewood. November 18, 1903.

123

A. E. Gallitan's Pope Toledo is a fine example of a handsome touring car. When motoring, the goggles, leather driving gloves and driving coat were all part of the necessary protective clothing.

Lakewood. 1904.

*With the top half down, younger members of the Strong family
pose in their new Columbia Electric Victoria.*

Dr. Charles Browne is seated behind the wheel of this two-seater
sports model Peerless. A common practice, Browne's initials
are visible on the side of the car beneath the young lady's arm rest.

Bb4027   Spring Lake. 1907.

In a beautifully decorated auto and with Spring Lake and Saint Catharine's
Memorial Church in the background, Mrs. A. B. Ryker and friend
are about to join other "automobilists" in a gala parade.

Ar1090   Spring Lake. 1905.

Two Boston Terriers seated beside him in a Waverly Electric, Charles C. Miller and Mrs. Miller (in a more formal vehicle) display six of their prized automobiles.

Winners in a Floral Parade, Mr. & Mrs. Charles C. Miller and friends pass proudly in review. Part of an eight-day Long Branch Auto Carnival, over two hundred vehicles gathered at the West End Hotel before the start of this event. A "prominent Cottager and Automobilist," Miller was a partner in the Peerless Rubber Company.

Am1035

Long Branch. August 26, 1905.

*William Proale's new American Mercedes on display. These cars were
assembled between 1904 and 1907 by the Daimler Manufacturing Company
of Long Island City, New York. This custom body was made by former
coach builders, J. M. Quinby & Sons of Newark, New Jersey.*

Ap1099

Spring Lake. 1905.

*Headly and Farmer's fully equipped chauffer-driven Packard
could readily be turned into an open touring car by unbuttoning
the canvas top. A dangling lantern (tail light) and rear trunks
explain the origin of these now common automotive terms.*

Bh3793

Long Branch. 1907.

Quite formally, Mrs. W. E. Strong peers from her chauffer-driven popular French Renault.

Bs4220

Rumson. 1907.

Another choice of Mrs. W. E. Strong was this English-built Napier. With its powerful engine and massive body it was an impressive automobile.

Bs4221a

Rumson. 1907.

Delicate veils provide an additional touch of fashion to these ladies hats. Scarves kept the hats of the younger girls in place. Light summer coats (dusters) are evident as well as a pair of goggles worn just for this picture. J. Loewer's car, a Rainier, was first manufactured in Flushing, New York, in 1905.

Bl4179

Spring Lake. 1907.

132

"Chinese Minister Wu and Christian Auto Group" are parked curb side in a rarely seen Welch.
Although trees were budding, this chilly Spring day called for heavy coats and a lap robe.
The Welch was produced in Pontiac, Michigan, from 1904 to 1909.

Bw4651

Possibly Lakewood. 1908.

Returning from the Elkwood Park auto races in what appears to be a Standard,
Mr. B. Hendricks and a friend pause near the boardwalk. The car is equipped
with "Goodrich Quick Detachable" tires.

Bh4933   Long Branch. 1909.

134

With the top down, a heavy driving coat, gloves, cap and goggles were needed to thoroughly enjoy a brisk winter's ride in I. A. Rosenthal's handsome Lozier.

Br4554

Lakewood. 1909.

Walter R. Patten's chauffer-driven entry won third prize in a two-day Carnival at Long Branch. Mrs. Thomas G. Patten is highly visible, but Mrs. Julia Roberts is all but obscured by floral decorations of white and pale green hydrangeas.

Bp4531b

Long Branch. August 21, 1909.

Clarence J. Hausman was awarded first prize (a cup donated by Bernard M. Baruch)
for the most original design in the novelty class. Hausman's automobile,
a reproduction of the Wright Brother's aeroplane,
was driven by aviator Richard Armstrong.

Bh4384

West End. August 21, 1909.

137

Sports cars, touring cars and a few horses and carriages complete a delightful view of the Deal Beach Casino during the summer of 1905.

A variety of cars (including Fords and Renaults) surround four horse-drawn carriages at the Elberon Station in 1913. The woman in the open touring car quietly reads a newspaper as a half dozen chauffeurs chat while awaiting the arrival of the next train.

Mae500

While photographing the site of a serious accident, George A. M. Morris,
in a lighter moment, posed the Central Railroad of New Jersey
investigating team for this obviously unofficial portrait.

Near Bridgewater, N.J. 1915.